Re-Me

(Reinvent Me)

Re-Me

REINVENT ME

Re-Me
Reinvent Me

Unless otherwise noted, Scripture quotations in this book are Taken from the following sources:

Holy Bible, New International Version.

Re-Me (Reinvent Me)

Downer, Teka

Re-Me/Teka Downer, 2013

Copyright © 2013 Teka Downer

ISBN 978-0-615-98588-6

www.remeteka.com

Re-Me
Reinvent Me

Preface

Re is a prefix, occurring originally in loan words from Latin, used with the meaning "again" or "again and again" to indicate repetition, or with the meaning "back" or "backward" to indicate withdrawal or backward motion.*(dictionary.com)* Re-Me, or Reinvent Me is all about becoming Me again! This may sound strange to become me again, but there is much truth to it. A couple of years ago, my Pastor preached a detailed series on identity. These messages were packed with information on being who God originally created you to be. He stressed the importance of getting back to your original mind, your God-given mind. He revealed the power in renewing your mind as revealed to us in Romans 12:2. Here we are told not to conform to the patterns of this world but to be transformed by the renewing of our minds. In this passage the Greek word for renewal is anakainosis which means to get back to the original mindset. This was no doubt a pivotal point in my life to fight for what I had lost, my original mind which held my true identity.

Foreword by Pastor Merritt

In life we often find ourselves defining life's past, present, and future by the things that are most memorable. Unfortunately, in most cases we remember the things that are catastrophic, or negative in nature. In the years I've spent pastoring, I've been on my own personal journey of understanding the damage of my personal past. As I counsel couples and individuals I'm learning that I'm not the only person needing to understand the effects and affects of the past. It literally shapes our self-talk.

We become so comfortable with toxic living that our self-talk makes us feel comfortable with less life. Over 2000 years ago God sent His only son to help us rethink ourselves and not define our present and our future by our past. Jesus taught that whatever we internalize, (that is in our thinking) we will externalize. Whatever we think, we will become. God sends individuals to remind us of ways to overcome our toxic thinking from generation to generation. I believe we have that in Teka Downer

Teka has masterfully captured what I believe to be a cutting edge method in overcoming the traumatic experiences and mistakes of our past. We have the power to undo everything we've done to ourselves by taking a good look at who we've become.

I encourage all to take seriously the Re-Me challenges as Teka has made this powerful process as colorful and lively as if you were having a personal life coaching session with the Re-life expert herself. Know that her methods are not based on abstract thoughts by theoretic principles, but rather personal experiences and her own life challenges. Enjoy the ride and celebrate the victory!

Pastor Esaias Merritt

Re-Me

Reinvent Me

Teka D.

Introduction

Truth is, right now in this very moment, I am writing this book from a place of real pain, real hurt, and real fear. My home is in what they call active foreclosure with no listed sale date as of yet (most aren't aware, not even my parents). I walked away from my job last year to begin a business that I never fully prepared for; I did walk off by faith, but oh to my surprise, Faith actually requires more than me believing things will happen but me spending some real quality time with the Lord to hear His direction. My best friend in the entire whole world is currently missing in action (he is alive, just newly in love) and my body is about 12 pounds lighter than it was two weeks ago. When I tell you I am here at rock bottom and have no idea why I am spilling the beans via paper and pen, I mean that with every fiber of my being! But God!

God gave me this whole Reinvent Me campaign about a month ago, a process to begin to motivate others to be better in their current circumstances. I began to promote it to a couple of my friends. Encourage *them* to live better and achieve more before the year ends. I never would have guessed *I* would be getting reinvented in such a matter. Well the truth of the matter is - He is doing it right now! That's right. I am finding healing and a reason to wake up each morning as we reinvent me together.

I asked Him to do it himself a long time ago, because He's God and He can do anything! But He said: This is our journey together. The word says for WITH God Nothing Shall be Impossible (Luke 1:37) so that's us together. He asked me to go ahead and invite some new-found friends along for the journey. So the fact that you are reading this makes you one of my new-found friends. Welcome to the Re-Me challenge.

Re-Me

Reinvent Me

I am not sure where you are in your life, perhaps things are great, just OK, or falling apart. Just know wherever you are in this particular moment; your life will only get better! I believe it with everything on the inside of me - you are going to be a better person before this journey ends. I don't know you, but please believe I love you and my prayers are with you as you take this 15-day challenge. Enjoy your journey friend, Re-Me, we will be better!

Contact me at www.remeteka.com and let's begin your journey to reinvention together

Re-Me
Challenge of the day

Time alone with the Father is where it all begins and ultimately where it is going to all end!

In everything you do today, find a way to have some quiet time **ALONE** with the Father. Whenever you get outside, whether it's early in the morning, noon day or as the moon is rising, focus on His marvelous works. Adore the sky and the moving clouds, watch as the birds soar effortlessly or the ants walk hurriedly. Know that all of it is a work from the Father's hand to be enjoyed by you. I'm always hopeful when I see birds flying. It is in that moment I am reminded of His word in Matthew 6:25-26, if He takes care of the birds that neither sow nor reap, surely He will take care of me. After spending time with the Father, write down your experiences.

_____
_____
_____
_____
_____
_____
_____
_____
_____
_____
_____
_____
_____
_____

Re-Me
Reinvent Me

_____

_____
_____
_____
_____
_____
_____
_____
_____
_____

Father God in Heaven, it is my prayer that you expose yourself to my friend on this day in a brand new way. Father, may nature come alive to your child as he/she is intentional about spending time alone with you. I pray that you guard his/her heart with your love as you share more of your creation with him/her. It is in the matchless name of Jesus we pray.

Why this challenge: Alone time with God is the most important and fundamental step when it comes to reinventing your current person. Why not find out from the Father who you really are since He is the one who created you. He knows everything about you even the stuff you are still learning about yourself!

Don't forget to work towards your goals.
Re-Me I will be better.

Re-Me
Challenge of the day
Dream, Dream, Dream!

I dare you today to **DREAM** again. Ask the Holy Spirit to remind you of your life's dreams once upon a time ago. So what's so wrong with dreaming anyway? Nothing! Often times in life we start off with great dreams; dreams of business startup, dreams of going back to school, or dreams of traveling the world. So what happens to our dreams? Life. Life comes out of nowhere and smacks us slap dab in the face and causes us to forget about our dreams. Well, not anymore, not today. We are reinventing ourselves and no one said this would be easy. I am asking that you take two days to focus on this challenge. **DREAM** again, then dream some more. Life is never too difficult for us to begin to dream again. Take a moment to write down some of your dreams.

_____

_____

_____

_____

_____

_____

_____

_____

_____

_____

_____

_____

_____

_____

_____

Re-Me
Reinvent Me

_____
_____
_____
_____
_____
_____
_____
_____

Father God in Heaven, I ask that you give us our dreams back. Lord I ask that you touch my friend right now in the midst of whatever fear or doubt of dreaming again may be surfacing. Lord, remind him/her that it is your will for us to have hope. Master, I pray that no matter how difficult or challenging life may be for them that you stir up the need for dreams in his/her life. We praise you and we thank you, for it is in the mighty name of Jesus we pray.

Why this challenge: Dreams are important, they serve as a road map to our hidden purpose. Without dreams we are without hope, without hope we live in disappointment. Dreams are instrumental in living a fulfilled life.

Don't forget to work towards your goals.
Re-Me I will be better.

Re-Me
Challenge of the day
Now Faith!

The last two days you have capitalized on your dreams. Now it is time to exercise **FAITH**. Not faith in people or things but **FAITH** in the Almighty Father. Simply put, if God said it, that settles it! There are no ifs, ands or buts about it, His word is final. So how do we find this **FAITH**? We search within; the word of God tells us that we have each been given a measure of **FAITH**. I am able to write this book due to the **FAITH** that is on the inside of me given me by God. It's not just in some of us, but all of us! Isn't that good news, it is just up to you to work your **FAITH**. Today, Read as many scriptures as you can about **FAITH**. I will leave you with a couple of my favorites: Matthew 17:20, Hebrews 11:20, Hebrews 11:6, and Romans 10:17. Write your thoughts about faith.

_____

_____

_____

_____

_____

_____

_____

_____

_____

_____

_____

_____

_____

_____

_____

Re-Me
Reinvent Me

_____

_____

_____

_____

_____

_____

_____

Father God in Heaven, we just praise and thank you for right now. Lord, we thank you that you have given each one of us our very own measure of faith and that you will instruct us as we walk by faith. Father, help my friend hear ever so clearly from you and see the manifestations of his/her Faith. Lord, help him/her to walk boldly in your word as he/she puts his/her belief into action. For it is in the mighty name of Jesus we pray, Amen.

Why this challenge: The Word of God tells us without FAITH it is impossible to please God. As with any parent/child relationship, the child seeks to please his/her parent(s). The more we get to know God as our loving Heavenly Father, the more we will desire to please Him.

Don't forget to work towards your goals.
Re-Me I will be better.

Teka D.

Re-Me
Challenge of the day
The Climb Out!

Have you ever been in a rough place? I mean a tough place emotionally and physically. Everything around you is just filled with despair. The sun is shining, yet the day feels so hopelessly bleak to you. No matter how much you try to explain this place of hurt no one ever truly understands where you are. Then you my friend have experienced *Destination Pit.* Pits can be very dark lonely places and to top it all off they can be slimy and slippery, making it almost impossible to get out. I want to encourage you and remind you of my introduction, I told you all where I was as I began writing this book. Well, I want you to know, I have full joy right now because I have experienced the climb **OUT**! That's right; I feel it right now in my life and declare it in yours. I felt the master reach for my hand, and I am climbing **OUT** of my dark place. I want you to know, you don't have to stay in that pit of confusion, worry, anger, depression, guilt, or deceit any longer. There is a greater power who wants to pull you **OUT** of darkness and expose His marvelous light unto you. Perhaps your pit isn't as severe as any of the things listed; your pit could be laziness, complacency, routine, or lack of follow through. Today I challenge you to identify your pit and begin the great and mighty climb OUT! Here are a couple of my favorite verses as it pertains to The Climb Out: Psalm 40:1-2 and 1 Peter 2:9 Write about the pit you either are currently experiencing or have experienced.

_____
_____
_____
_____

Re-Me
Reinvent Me

Father God in Heaven, on this day I ask that your mighty hand guide and lift my friend into a place that is higher than right now. Father, show him/her the might of your hand as you lift him/her out of comfortable places. Remind him/her that you hold his/her future in your hand so there is no need to continue in despair. Lord, for my friend who is praying this prayer, I ask that you move in a mighty way in his/her life right now. We praise you and we thank you, for it is in the mighty name of Jesus we pray.

Why this challenge: God loves all of us and it hurts him to see us in despair or complacency. He has a great purpose that He wants each one of us to realize and obtain. Your way OUT is your way up as you connect to His purpose.

Don't forget to work towards your goals.
Re-Me I will be better.

Teka D.

Re-Me
Challenge of the day
Establish The Relationship(s)!

"Life moves at the speed of relationships" -Mayor Hardie Davis. One day I was having lunch with two brilliant minds discussing our roles and partnerships in our community. We discussed the challenges of providing new-age leaders with the skills necessary to advance in their current careers. The key ingredient that we all came up with - as it pertains to achieving any level of success in the business world, Faith community, and personal- social aspects - was relationships. As I quoted earlier, "life moves at the speed of relationships." This is a clear indicator that there are people you need to **ESTABLISH** relationships with to help you reach and meet your goals. Why reinvent the wheel when someone has already created it for you? Why not sit down with the creator of the wheel one day for lunch, and find out how that creation came about! Today I challenge you to tap into that dream you desire to achieve and begin to **ESTABLISH** the right relationship with someone who knows or can help you achieve your dream. Write about some relationships you desire to establish.

_____
_____
_____
_____
_____
_____
_____
_____
_____

14

Re-Me
Reinvent Me

_____
_____
_____
_____
_____
_____
_____
_____
_____

Father God in Heaven, I ask that you help my friend as he/she begins to tap into his/her dreams and establish the right relationships in achieving his/her dreams. Father, let them know that you can do anything and that you have already prepared his/her path, fixed with the right people to help advance his/her dreams. Oh, that you would show him/her today who to connect with. We praise you and we thank you, for it is in the mighty name of Jesus we pray.

Why this challenge: We can't make it here alone, we need each other. Relationships are the heartbeat of life. Relationships have literally helped form me into who I am today.

Don't forget to work towards your goals.
Re-Me I will be better.

Teka D.

Re-Me
Challenge of the day
Push Beyond Right Now!

You are more than your **RIGHT** now. You are more than
hurt, worries, failures, and disappointments. You are more
than this moment. I want to challenge you to see yourself
beyond your current state of mind. Beyond your current
successes or failures, push beyond **RIGHT** now and see
yourself through your years. We have already talked about
dreams and faith, both ingredients are key to being able to
visualize your future. Without dreams or vision we perish, we
have nothing to look forward to, so we simply exist. **PUSH**
beyond your current contentment with your decent job, or
your current contentment with your average body weight.
PUSH and get into a place that overwhelms your current
condition and demands your very best. Write about right
now.

Re-Me
Reinvent Me

_____

_____
_____
_____
_____
_____
_____
_____
_____

Father God in Heaven, help my friend to push beyond right now, his/her current fears, current failures, and even current successes. Father, I ask that you help my friend see that there is so much more to life than this current phase. We praise you and we thank you, for it is in the mighty name of Jesus we pray.

Why this challenge: Pushing beyond right now is essential in creating a healthy lifestyle. Without the ability to look forward to more, we simply just exist. To simply just exist goes against who our Father is and who He created us to be. The word of God tells us that all creation is waiting on us! Creation is waiting on you to tap into who you are, and not just who you are right now. (Romans 8:19)

Don't forget to work towards your goals.
Re-Me I will be better.

Re-Me
Challenge of the day

Think on the Impossible!

Ever had something you desired but it looked completely impossible to achieve? Today I dare you to **THINK** on the impossible. That's right - change your current state of thinking and **THINK** on the impossible. Start daydreaming right now on that impossible task, but this time **THINK** of yourself achieving the absolute impossible. The word of God tells us as a man thinks, so is he. (Proverbs 23:7) So ultimately thinking about overcoming the impossible will make you the ultimate overcomer. Write about the impossible in your life.

_____
_____
_____
_____
_____
_____
_____
_____
_____
_____
_____
_____
_____
_____
_____
_____

Re-Me
Reinvent Me

_____
_____
_____
_____
_____
_____
_____
_____

Father God in Heaven, remind my friend right now of your word that proclaims with you nothing shall be impossible. Encourage him/her in knowing that you can make all things possible according to his/her belief. Stretch him/he today to aim for the impossible in you and see the manifestations. We praise you and we thank you, for it is in the mighty name of Jesus we pray.

Why this challenge: The word of God tells us God is able to do exceedingly abundantly more than we could think or ask. So if we see it as impossible, the word of God tells us God can go above and beyond what we see. With God the impossible is possible, simply because He is God Almighty. (Ephesians 3:20)

Don't forget to work towards your goals.
Re-Me I will be better.

Re-Me
Challenge of the day

Who's in your circle?

A couple of days ago we discussed the importance of relationships for professional gain. Today let's focus on those relationships that have helped you overcome all sorts of personal strife. **WHO'S** in your circle, who are the people that support you the most? Envision these people today and begin to praise God for them. I mean have a fit thanking God for them! List their names below and pray for each one of them intently. In the book of Job, Job experienced great hardship and a lot of that hardship came from some of his close friends. But it wasn't until Job prayed for his friends that the Lord released the blessings in his life. Identify **WHO's** who and pray for them. I understand your life may not be in the best shape, but there is a power that gets released when we pray for others.

_____
_____
_____
_____
_____
_____
_____
_____
_____
_____
_____
_____
_____

Re-Me
Reinvent Me

_____

_____
_____
_____
_____
_____
_____

Father God in Heaven, guard our hearts and our minds as
we pray for those people who are in our inner circle. Father,
give us a renewed strength as we thank you for bringing
these people into our lives and fulfilling whatever roles you
have designed for them to. We ask that you send mighty
blessings their way on this day. We praise you and we thank
you, for it is in the mighty name of Jesus we pray.

Why this challenge: Sometimes it is so easy to focus on
what we don't have and what we want; often times we
forget about others. There is a special power that gets
released when we are mindful of others.

Don't forget to work towards your goals.
Re-Me I will be better.

Re-Me
Challenge of the day
Challenge Yourself!

Today you are your own challenge! Challenge **YOURSELF** to be better today than you were yesterday! If you had an OK day yesterday, challenge **YOURSELF** to make today incredible. No one can reinvent you like you. What were the things that worried you yesterday? What were the things that had you down? Whatever they were don't think *on* them but think *above* them today. Thinking about yesterday's worries is just like wearing yesterday's outfit today and in the famous words of Sweet Brown, "AIN'T NOBODY GOT TIME FOR THAT!" Write all about how today will be an amazing day for you.

_____
_____
_____
_____
_____
_____
_____
_____
_____
_____
_____
_____
_____
_____

Re-Me
Reinvent Me

_____
_____
_____
_____
_____
_____
_____
_____
_____

Father God in Heaven, I ask that you help my friends to be better today than they were yesterday. Lord, remind him/her that they ARE in control of their day. Master, I pray that no matter how difficult or challenging life may be for them currently, you give them power to be better right now. We praise you and we thank you, for it is in the mighty name of Jesus we pray.

Why this challenge: We are a little more than half way through with the Re-Me process. It is my sincere hope that every day you are finding yourself better than the previous day. This challenge ensures that you make today better than yesterday on purpose.

Don't forget to work towards your goals.
Re-Me I will be better.

Teka D.

Re-Me
Challenge of the day
Take a Step back!

The other day I had a friend speak to me about his
frustrations while taking a drawing class. In this class he had
to draw an object as it was on display in front of the
classroom. This was hard for him because he had no prior
drawing experience. He told me how in the midst of his
drawing he would get so angry because it looked nothing
like the object in front of the classroom. Until he decided to
take a step **BACK**, once he stepped **BACK** he could see how
his drawing and the object matched perfectly - to his surprise!
Your life may look like a bunch of chaos right now, but today
I challenge you to take a step **BACK** and really assess your
life. Perspective is everything, change your thinking, change
your life. Write about this challenge as you take a step back.

_____
_____
_____
_____
_____
_____
_____
_____
_____
_____
_____
_____
_____
_____

Re-Me
Reinvent Me

_____
_____
_____
_____
_____
_____
_____
_____
_____
_____

Father God in Heaven, oh that you would help us all to take a step back right now; help us to realize we may not have all we desire but nonetheless you have kept us. Father, expand our vision as we take a step back. Show us the many victories you have already won on our behalf. We praise you and we thank you, for it is in the mighty name of Jesus we pray.

Why this challenge: A quick step back can cause you to reflect on past accomplishments versus the current deficit. Perspective is everything, change your thinking, change your life.

Don't forget to work towards your goals.
Re-Me I will be better.

Teka D.

Search Within!

I once expressed to my son about this great movie I hoped to show him one day. The title of it: "The Parent Trap." I told him how I used to watch it all the time as a little girl and I wanted him to watch it with me some day. The other day I was cleaning our entertainment system and came upon that very movie! I had no idea I even owned the movie. I mean the whole time, my favorite movie sat collecting dust right up under my nose. What precious treasure do you have tucked away in the corner of your mind? Today I am challenging you to **SEARCH** within. Are you a secretly skilled organizer, a dynamic leader? You will never know until you **SEARCH** within.

_____
_____
_____
_____
_____
_____
_____
_____
_____
_____
_____
_____
_____
_____

Re-Me
Reinvent Me

_____
_____
_____
_____
_____
_____
_____
_____

Father God in Heaven, today we want to thank you for who
you have created us to be. Lord, we understand that we
have been created in your image. So, today we ask that you
reveal us to ourselves, show us the wonderful treasures we
possess on the inside. We praise you and we thank you, for it
is in the mighty name of Jesus we pray.

Why this challenge: It is so important to know what you
are made of and what special skills you possess. My mom
always says if you know better, you will do better.

Don't forget to work towards your goals.
Re-Me I will be better.

Re-Me
Challenge of the day
Commit to it!

One of my favorite scriptures says "**COMMIT** to the Lord whatever you do and your plans will succeed." Proverbs 16:3. Whatever it is that you want to be better at, make sure that you are **COMMIT**ed to seeing it through. Commitment takes time and sacrifice and a lot of willingness on your part. If you are committed to seeing a habit broken, then you will know that commitment will take time. I just love how Proverbs 16:3 gives so much hope! I have learned, if I **COMMIT** my plans wholeheartedly unto the Lord they most assuredly every time succeed. How about you **COMMIT** to it and give it a try.

_____
_____
_____
_____
_____
_____
_____
_____
_____
_____
_____
_____
_____
_____
_____
_____
_____

Re-Me
Reinvent Me

_____
_____
_____
_____
_____
_____
_____
_____
_____

Father God in Heaven, help us today to honor our commitments unto you. Father, show us how to not only state your word, but be committed to being doers as well. Establish in us today a new level of commitment and allow us to see your successes. We praise you and we thank you, for it is in the mighty name of Jesus we pray.

Why this challenge: Commitment is challenging in itself. Most people are afraid of committing because they are afraid of failure. God did not give us the spirit of fear, so understand commitment is a daily task worth being fulfilled.

Don't forget to work towards your goals.
Re-Me I will be better.

Teka D.

Re-Me
Challenge of the day
Who are you?

Have you really asked yourself this question? Who are **YOU**, who did God create **YOU** to be? Many of us walk around day in and day out with no real knowledge of who God has created us to be. Most of us walk around defeated, living a sub-par life and can't even imagine our life being any better than its current state. Today I want to challenge you to answer this question, who are **YOU**? Do you know there is purpose all on the inside of **YOU**? You were created on purpose, so why aren't you living on purpose? Could it be because you have yet to discover this answer? Take some real time today and ask the Father to reveal you to you, write about your revelation.

_____
_____
_____
_____
_____
_____
_____
_____
_____
_____
_____
_____

Re-Me
Reinvent Me

Father God in Heaven, I thank you for your word which tells us we can come to you and ask anything and you will give us the knowledge we need. Father, right now I ask that you help my friend today to discover who you have called him/her to be. Lord, help them to see beyond right now and take you at your word. Please make it ever so clear and reveal their steps to becoming who you say they are. We praise you and we thank you, for it is in the mighty name of Jesus we pray.

Why this challenge: Knowing who you are can help get you where you need to be. God tells us He knew us before we were formed in our mother's womb, why not ask Him who you are.

Don't forget to work towards your goals.
Re-Me I will be better.

Re-Me
Challenge of the day
Appreciate your journey!

I don't know about you, but this has been some **JOURNEY** for me! This whole reinvent me process has really shifted my way of thinking, challenged me beyond belief, and strengthened my relationship with the Father. Yet I wouldn't change one thing about this **JOURNEY**, because in the process I have found me, a reinvented me. I told you all earlier in this book I began writing from such a broken place, well I want you to know the Lord has fully restored me. He gave me back all I lost, with interest! I stand today telling you this **JOURNEY** has not been in vain. What about your journey, can you appreciate where you are right now, knowing, He can and will do the impossible. I am a living witness, the sooner you find something about your **JOURNEY** to appreciate, the sooner a new **JOURNEY** will unfold. Take time today to celebrate something on your current journey. You may not be where you *want* to be, but praise God, you are not where you *used* to be.

_____

_____

_____

_____

_____

_____

_____

_____

_____

Re-Me

Reinvent Me

_____

_____

_____

_____

_____

_____

_____

_____

_____

Father God in Heaven, we thank you for our journeys. No matter how rough, how hard, how impossible they may seem, we thank you for them. Lord, your word encourages us that you will work all things together for the good of they that love you according to your purpose. So we say thank you that even our current journeys are working for our good. Father, show my friends today your mighty hand and give them light for their current journey, for it is in the mighty name of Jesus we pray.

Why this challenge: A lot of the older saints in my church would always say, "I wouldn't take *nothing* for my journey now." They were simply saying the lessons learned were so incredibly valuable. It was during the tough journeys they learned of God's faithfulness, His love, and His compassion. I too concur.

Don't forget to work towards your goals.
Re-Me I will be better.

Re-Me
Challenge of the day
Time alone with the Father is where it all begins and ultimately where it all ends!

Wow! We have come to the end of our reinvent me journey together. I am so incredibly hopeful that you, like me, are in such an amazing point in your life at the completion of this book. We began by saying spend time with the Father. I will end by saying spend time with the Father. It is my sincere hope that it is no longer a hard thing to do. I pray that it is as natural as putting your clothes on at this point. One thing this whole Re-Me journey has taught me is that I desperately need time with my Heavenly Father. I learned throughout this journey there is no way I can make it without Him. Without Him I just exist. I believe with every ounce of my being that I was purposed to write this book and help you to become a better you. Now, as you continue your Re-Me journey without me, because you know this is a continual process, I pray that your prayer time excites you like never before. I pray that you rush in to get into the presence of the Father as if your life depended on it. And of course I pray that goodness and mercy shall follow you all the days of your life.

_____
_____
_____
_____
_____
_____

Re-Me
Reinvent Me

_____

_____
_____
_____
_____
_____
_____
_____
_____
_____
_____
_____
_____

Father God in Heaven, thank you for the many challenges you have brought our way. Thank you for building us up as only you can do. Lord, it is my sincere prayer that we are better. Better for you, better workers for your kingdom and better people for our families and within our communities. Father, I pray we see better, live better, and desire better. Thank you for reinventing us with your purpose. We praise you and we thank you, for it is in the mighty name of Jesus we pray, Amen.

Don't forget to work towards your goals.
Re-Me I will be better.

Re-Me

Reinvent Me

---

www.ingramcontent.com/pod-product-compliance
Lightning Source LLC
Chambersburg PA
CBHW072056040426
42447CB00012BB/3147